FAITH
Behind the Blue Wall
Finding God's Love and Divine Purpose
in Law Enforcement

D0066689

CLARENCE HINES

outskirtspress
DENVER, COLORADO

Outskirts Press, Inc.
http://www.outskirtspress.com

ISBN: 978-1-4787-4144-2

Outskirts Press and the "OP" logo are trademarks belonging to Outskirts Press, Inc.

PRINTED IN THE UNITED STATES OF AMERICA

Scripture Reference

"Truly I tell you, with no one in Israel have I found such faith" (Matthew 8:10 ESV).

Acknowledgments

I dedicate *Faith behind the Blue Wall* to my precious and loving wife Julia. No one has inspired me more than you. Your selfless encouragement gave me the strength to start and complete what I knew God was calling and enabling me to do. I cherish your sweet spirit, and I'm forever grateful for your prayers and early-morning forehead kisses. God has worked through all of our tears over the years and brought us safely to this point. I love you as Christ loves the church. Thank you for being my wife and my best friend.

Pastor Mary Thomas, my dear friend and mentor. Thank you for your wise counsel and for being a friend and confidante during the times I really needed a shoulder to cry on. Thanks for teaching us how important it is to love broken people. You mean the world to Julia and me, and we love you forever.

Pastor Carl S. Smith, thank you for all of your love, support, and encouragement as I prayerfully pondered retirement from the SLMPD. Thanks for the many wonderful life lessons in such a short time and loving me as a son. Thanks for believing in me and giving us a safe place to call home during a season of transition. We will forever be grateful to the New Beginning Church family for your love to our family. We love you, Pop Smith!

I also want to thank Lt. Adrienne Bergh of the St. Louis Metropolitan Police Department. Thank you always for your encouraging words and support. I will always remember our special bond and how much you supported my family and me during our time together in narcotics.

Lastly, Coach Joe Myers, words can't express the respect and admiration I have for you. The 4 years I spent as your assistant at Tower Grove Christian School were 4 of the best years of my life. Thanks for all of your love, support, and wisdom. Thanks for modeling Christ for me. You rock!

Contents

Foreword by Thomas Brewer

What does it mean to live your "Faith behind the Blue Wall"? As you read the pages of this book you will discover incredible insights about being a law enforcement officer as you walk through biblical accounts. If you are looking for a book that is simple to read, yet will challenge your thought process, then *this* book is for you!

There are very few books which capture my attention from the beginning. Many times I will have to read several pages, and even chapters, before I really begin to enjoy the book. That is not the case with this book.

From the start of this book, you will be drawn into the stories which Clarence Hines shares as he begins the journey as a young boy wanting to serve and protect. When I read the Introduction, I knew that I did not want to put this book down. You will begin to think you're in his grandpa's store years ago as he begins this journey.

Serving in law enforcement as a chaplain for the past 12 years, and now as a commissioned law enforcement officer, I have seen books written for our "tribe," meaning the law enforcement family. Never have I read a book which I believe will help and positively impact officers, their families, and the community like this book. Many times we go home, and as we lay in bed we place on our nightstand calls that affected us from that shift. If we never deal with them, over time, the "stack" will continue to grow with other calls, our responses, or the images we cannot forget. At some point, that "stack" will fall off the nightstand, and we must truly deal with everything we placed there over the years. Many times when this "stack" falls, our marriages fall apart, we lose our badges because we lost control in a use of force, or we abuse substances in order to try to suppress that stack on the nightstand. If you are currently serving as an officer or are retired, READ THIS BOOK. Don't just read it, but apply what is discussed in it to your life. You will truly be a better officer, spouse, parent, partner, and servant of the community if you embrace this book.

I also believe if you are married to an officer, have an officer in your family, or just know an officer, you should read this book. It will help you better understand what the officer is facing each time he or she places that badge on their chest and walks out the door.

As you read these pages, you will discover that the Bible addresses the very issues that law enforcement officers face each day. Join Clarence on this incredible journey of discovering what God desires for law enforcement officers!

Thomas E. Brewer
Law Enforcement Officer and Chaplain
President of ProActive Faith Ministries, Inc.
Author of *God Moments In Time*

Introduction

For many are called but few are chosen
(Matthew 22:14 ESV).

I can remember it just like it was yesterday. I was 7 years old at the time, and I was a very normal child, full of life, innocence, and vigor, as most 7 year olds are. My grandpa Bennie owned the local corner store which also served as the neighborhood hangout. I was proud my grandpa owned and ran his own business. It gave me a sense of pride and hope, even in a neighborhood of hopelessness. He would occasionally allow me to earn a honey bun or bag of chips by tearing down boxes. Mostly, it was where I often hung out, listened, and observed the older neighborhood men as they talked about everything from girls, jokes, and even how to commit crimes and get away with it. My grandpa's corner store is where I received my education to street life and picked up on the skills that would later serve me well in my call to a life of community service in law enforcement. I was enamored with the daily excitement of the corner store, which included dice games, pool tournaments, nearby drug sales, and even prostitution. I saw it all and was like a sponge soaking it all up. It may be hard to understand, but I never felt like I was in any real danger. Truth is, I didn't worry about it much. It was home.

Anyway, it seemed most of the older people in the neighborhood went out of their way to ensure I was protected and stayed on the right side of the law. A couple of my uncles, who were neck deep in the rackets, would often threaten me in an attempt to scare me away from "the life" (crime). They didn't have to worry, though. By the grace of God, there was never any part of me that wanted to be like the men from the old neighborhood. I was never drawn to their lifestyle, although I cared for a lot of them. I always had an unsettling inner feeling like I was called to stop them from doing wrong. I never talked about it, though. That was not the sort of thing you said in the neighborhood I grew up in.

My feelings were fully manifested one day when two men running from the police ran into my grandpa's store to take up refuge in the back storage area. They had apparently led the police on a high-speed chase and abandoned the stolen car after crashing. When the police came looking for them, as was usually the case, there were no witnesses willing to talk. Everyone in and around the store became quiet. The police detectives, with a disappointed look, were preparing to leave when to their surprise, they discovered there was one witness in the store. That witness was me. I knew I couldn't let them get away with running from the police. I mean, the police were my heroes, and they needed my help. I looked up to them and wanted to be like them. I stepped from behind the counter as they were about to exit the front door and said just loud enough for the detectives to hear me, "Excuse me, Officers, the two men you're looking for are hiding in the back room." With every eye in the store (and there must have been 20 to 30 people) now staring at me in sheer disappointment that I had violated the "no snitching" street code, I knew I had done the right thing, and it felt so incredibly good to help the police. I realized at that moment that I wanted to dedicate my life to helping others by pursuing justice through community service. As it turned out, what I was feeling that day was real. I guess you could say that I didn't become a police officer by accident. Considering the danger and demands of the work, I don't believe any of us do.

I lived faithfully, successfully, and safely behind the blue wall community for 21 years. Although now retired, I sit reflectively in a posture of looking with star-glazed eyes at the heroic feats of the men and women who wear the badge. They are forever my heroes, and I know God is well pleased with his law enforcement servants.

It is my prayer that I have built up enough equitable trust within the law enforcement community that you will open your heart to read and embrace God's loving care in the pages that follow.

This book is written to help law enforcement officers connect with the heart of God, through his infinite grace, as they serve their country and communities. It is also written to help law enforcement families understand the depth of God's love for his agents of justice. It is my sincere hope that helping families connect to the reality that God works through their love ones to accomplish his plans for mankind, will give them peaceful days and restful nights while their loved ones are on duty. Although law enforcement officers may seem distant at times, I hope that families will see the need to undergird these officers with much-needed support, love, and encouragement, no matter the situation.

Lastly, this book is written for the larger community to build bridges and promote reconciliation and healing in our communities. What communities really desire in their police force is transparency and partnership. By illuminating God's love and divine will for strong communities and positive police/community relations, this book ultimately is designed to tear down the walls of perceived tyranny and hostility and promote tolerance, healing, reconciliation, and restoration between law enforcement and the community at large.

Attention All Cars

The modern police force as we know it did not exist in Rome and the Ancient Near East. The Roman army carried out the duties of our modern-day police officers. While their stories have been largely overlooked in scripture throughout history, their stories are our stories and have life-changing value for the law enforcement community. God's love for law enforcement officers and his commitment to justice and mercy are illustrated through their stories in this book.

Whenever I mention the law enforcement community in this book, I want to be clear that I am not only referring to police officers, but to the broader law enforcement community as well. Law enforcement covers a broad spectrum of dedicated crime-fighting specialists and their families, including local and federal law enforcement, military, private security officers, corrections officers, civilians, and support personnel.

Law enforcement is a tight-knit private community. It's not located on a map; one cannot find it by searching high and low. The police community is located in the threads of uniformed symbolism and the foundational principles of honor, integrity, fairness, and service. It is our collective bond through a commitment to justice that unites our hearts in shared fellowship, trust, and camaraderie. This is the most private of communities where families are embraced and the men and women who wear the uniform become family. The police community is a special place, not a perfect place. It is a part of larger society and therefore, can fall victim to the same ills that plague so much of our world. Satan and his legions of fallen angels are hard at work in the police communities, similar to that in larger society, except, I think, he works harder at tempting our heroes behind the badge. As you engage this book, may you find help, hope, and healing in its pages . . .

CHAPTER 1

A Revisit to Hallowed Ground

Those who reject the law praise the wicked,
but those who keep the law [law enforcement]
strive against them (Proverbs 28:4 ESV).

I honestly don't remember much about the day class 91-1 was sworn in as police officers officially. I was too excited to hit the streets and begin doing some good. One of my regrets in my career is that I wish I had allowed the words of the oath to penetrate my heart a little deeper. I wish I would have had more time to allow the words to permeate and resonate in the deepest parts of my being. While I'm certainly comfortable that I lived out my oath to the best of my ability, I'm sad that it took me over 20 years to do a revisit to something that is foundationally so important for a lawman.

Without question, the police officers' oath is hallowed ground. The final words of the oath ("so help me God") bear witness to this truth. While most of us may not even remember the last words of the oath, it encourages me that it ends with a plea to the divine for help in carrying out each and every precept. I'm even more encouraged at how faithful God has been to each state and federal officer in fulfilling the promises of faithful service to the community. You may not think about it much, but God has promised protection to the community from wicked and evil people. Our faithfulness to our oath allows us to be a conduit for the manifested presence of God and fulfilled promises of protection to a broken and hurting world. That's why I believe today that it is important to revisit our oath periodically to fortify and reaffirm our commitment to justice and mercy.

We are an integral part of God's justice system. We are not the whole of it; however, we are the beginning of the justice wheel. Our call, our mandate, is to find those who violate the laws and bring them before the courts to be tried without prejudice.

Whenever my team was preparing to execute a search warrant in the Narcotics Unit I supervised, I used to tell the detectives that worked for me that I believed we were God's response to the prayer requests for help from someone who lived on the block of our target address. I believed it then and still believe it very deeply today. There are people like my grandmother who believed that if you ask God for help in prayer, he's going to respond. You know what? My grandmother was right! God does respond, and at just the right time.

Ultimately, the God of justice is faithful to help those who pray for his help and those who may not. That's what grace is. In his righteous and loving character, God helps and blesses us, even though we may not deserve his help. From God's perspective, he wants us at our best physically, mentally, and spiritually. As we will see later, he's our partner in law enforcement and has not left us to fend for ourselves.

Here is a sample oath for you to do your own revisit. It is

my prayer that it will be a humbling reminder of the enormity of our call and our deep need for God's help as we go about protecting and serving his precious people in the community.

A sample oath of a law enforcement pledge may read as, "I, (your name), do solemnly swear that I will support the Constitution of the (country), and the Constitution of the state of (your state). I will faithfully and impartially discharge and perform all the duties of a police officer of the (your agency) to the best of my ability, so help me God."

CHAPTER **#2**

Knocking Out Superman

When He told them, "I am He," the law enforcement officers
stepped back and fell to the ground (John 18:6 ESV).

I called this chapter "Knocking Out Superman" because
as a young man surrounded by criminal elements and danger,
police officers were my heroes and I wanted to be just like
them. I admired even then what they represented and what
they stood for. They were my Superman.

Unlike some of the comic book characters, they don't
wear funny-looking costumes with cool logos stitched in; they
wear uniforms. They don't wear big letters on their chests,
such as a big "P" for policeman; they wear shiny badges as a
symbol of their heroic status.

When I was a young man growing up on the north side
of St. Louis in the 5th police district, surrounded by drugs
and the criminal element, the police officers walking the beat
always made me feel safe and gave me a sense of profound
hope and something to aspire to. Even at age 7, I can dis-
tinctly remember their shiny badges, blue nylon pants with
the white piping down the sides, dark shades, and their bushy

mustaches. Unfortunately, many people in the old neighborhood wanted to celebrate the criminal element, but not me; I wanted to be "police." On one sunny afternoon, I can still remember the now-retired Detective Sergeant Donald King emerging from the east alley of John and Blair with a large .357 Magnum at his side, looking for a couple of wanted suspects. I was frozen, and I could not move or breathe.

On another occasion, I can remember the now-retired Lt. Michael Barnes pummeling the neighborhood tough guy on a disturbance call that had gone bad. In that same incident, I got to see my first officer in need of "aid call" and quickly learned that when an officer needs help, they all come running. When they show up, they intend to win.

Without any real heroes to look up to, the police officers of the St. Louis Metro Police Department were my early inspiration. I loved what they represented and what they stood for. They represented everything I was feeling inside but didn't really know how to explain at the time. I didn't want to be a Marvel superhero like all the other kids in the neighborhood. I wanted to be "police." They were my "Superman"!

Law enforcement officers wear uniforms as an identifying symbol and continuous reminder that courageous men and women stand ready to do battle on behalf of the community. Unlike our fictional caped crusader friends, law enforcement officers are real. They are the ones who have been divinely placed in our society to take care of us. It has become a fundamental truth in my life and in the lives of my family members that police officers will always be our heroes.

In spite of the inherent authority and power given to law enforcement to carry out our duties, there is a force more powerful than our heroes in blue. A power that is clearly evident in John's Gospel. In a climactic chain of events, Roman police officers, aided by the first recorded criminal informant, Judas Iscariot, and under the watchful eye of the political elite, went to arrest Jesus of Nazareth and bring him in for questioning on trumped-up charges. After their informant, Judas, had identified Jesus with a kiss on the cheek, the officers turned their attention toward Jesus. Jesus, fully aware of the situation, demonstrated not only his gracious and high regard for law enforcement and justice, but also his power over the government and judicial system. Knowing that he was about to be arrested, Jesus, in a cooperative tone that still resonates in scripture, displays genuine respect for the police in helping them to do their jobs. Contextually, it would have been like arresting a local celebrity for the officers, I suppose. Law enforcement does not get to pick and choose who they arrest.

Jesus asked very simply, "Whom do you seek?" They answered, "We seek Jesus of Nazareth." When he told them, "I am he," the police officers all stepped back and fell to the ground (John 18:6). Jesus did not resist arrest or try to assault the officers. In fact, he did nothing as the arresting officers involuntarily fell to the ground. The involuntary reaction to the power of Jesus' authoritative words and power alone is stunning and a clear illustration of his power over all of creation. The officers, ever diligent in their duties, after overcoming interference from one of Jesus' disciples, Peter, were finally able to arrest Jesus without further incident.

Feeling the pressure from the political and social elite, as far as the officers were concerned, I suppose it didn't matter who Jesus was (although they didn't fully know who he was at the time). A complaint had been made of a law violation and the officers moved in and did their jobs. Imagine going home to tell your family, "Hey, guys, I arrested God today." Crickets!

This is an encouraging story for me, and I hope you can find encouragement in knowing that while you have been adorned with arrest powers and authority from the state, as well as gifts and talents from the hand of God, God is infinitely more powerful than the law enforcement community. That should humble us. I have come to realize how blessed we are when I consider that same power that caused the officers to involuntarily fall is the same gracious power that covers and keeps us as we police the community. That same power is able to give us peace in the midst of inevitable trials, heartbreaks, and setbacks. It's in the grace of that power that we can be strengthened and find forgiveness for not always being perfect, even though the community expects us to be. The power to be over comers and victors in life is found by grace through faith in a personal relationship with the same Jesus who daily continues to show his love, respect, and high regard for what we do every day as law enforcement officers. His power is always available, for if you are searching, he may always be found.

CHAPTER **#3**

The Call to Serve Family
(Why our service should start here)

"Your wife will be like a fruitful vine within your house; your children will be like olive shoots around your table"
(Psalm 128:3 ESV).

Having been a part of the law enforcement community for the past 21 years has been the greatest of privileges but has also taught me many life lessons. Most of them I had to learn the old-fashioned hard way. Aren't those the best lessons? The lessons where, in the end, we can clearly see God's gracious and divine hand shaping and growing us.

As I think about my many observations over the years regarding police life, there is one gut-wrenching observation: police life can be devastating on families, mostly because of chronic stress. Studies have shown that dealing with chronic stressful situations can take its toll on even the most seasoned law enforcement officers. I can tell you from my own personal experience that an officer's family life can slowly and steadily erode over time. If left unchecked, one day you wake up and realize that you and your family have become strangers. You really can't put your finger on it, but you know things are not quite right. There is a distinct tendency for officers to shut down emotionally and distance themselves from family members. We tend to feel like it is our safe place at the time. I did it without really realizing what was going on. I can tell you one thing for sure . . . I knew something wasn't right, and I knew that my family was in trouble, just by the way my wife and son looked at me. It actually got to the point that they *didn't* look at me, they looked *through* me. They were not proud of what I had become. I had become controlling, mean-spirited, distant, and when confronted, defensive.

The reality is that I am still trying to rebuild some of the brokenness in my own family, particularly with my son, created by the harsh realities of serving a community as police and all that it entails. For years, I was sinking because I didn't understand what was going on and because of the police culture of never displaying weakness. When I finally admitted to myself that I was a mess inside, I really didn't know where to turn for help. I didn't feel like there was anyone I could open up to.

You know, it's interesting. Those in law enforcement have all had the unfortunate instance of having to arrest or deal with a teenage or adult child of a police officer who had somehow lost his or her way. Some of us have had to make those tough phone calls to colleagues in the middle of the night to tell them that we were holding their child for drugs or illegal weapons possession, or even shoplifting and/or underage drinking. This is uncomfortable to say, but it needs to be stated emphatically. Here's the truth. While there are many who have managed to find that perfect balance between serving their families and their call to serve the community, there are, unfortunately, too many in law enforcement that are excellent at what they do every day publicly, but who are failing at home privately. It's great that everyone at work in your agency thinks you are amazing at what you do. That's great; however, we should never put too much stock in what those outside of our primary family unit have to say about us. If you really want to get a status check, find out what your spouse, children, mother, or father think about you. How do they really feel about you? Do they quietly hate to see you coming home some days? Do they feel that you are serving your family as well as you are policing the community or have you made them accept the fact that they are second fiddle?

Here's a larger question. Is it possible to be a fearless, great, and respected warrior of service and justice at work and be so consumed with defending a city or nation that you look up one day and realize your family has become dysfunctional? Of course, the answer to that question is a resounding "yes!" Whenever we consider the life of the great King David of the Bible, many are often surprised to learn that such a God-fearing, mighty warrior, fearless leader, and defender of a nation could have such a dysfunctional family at home. When I say "dysfunctional," I mean to the tenth degree. So let's run down the list as we examine this in a law enforcement context.

For starters, David chose to have an affair with one of his neighbors who was the wife of one of his faithful officers. Not only did she become pregnant, David ensured the officer was assigned to the roughest part of town with limited resources, during peak crime hours, with no backup, where the officer was certain to be killed. It was sort of like an indirect ambush. Additionally, David's children were disrespectful and rebellious. One son, Absalom, tried to kill him. Another son, Amnon, raped his half sister Tamar. His son Absalom, enraged by the rape of his sister and because his father David, who was apparently too busy at work, did nothing, killed his brother Amnon for raping Tamar. David had apparently become so indifferent to his son Absalom, that in a desperate move for attention, he tried to kill David, his father. Whew! A good question to ask is, could David have prevented this unfortunate chain of events in his own household? I believe David would be the first to admit that he made many personal mistakes as a father. What his children needed most was love, time, safety, and personal attention from their father. As we will see below, it would have made all the difference.

One of the really cool things about God is that he engages us through the biblical story line to show us that we are not alone in having to wrestle with the challenges of trying to balance our jobs with the demands of family life. It encourages me that David, one of my personal biblical heroes, struggled with some of the same issues as I. It was through the deep brokenness and dysfunction of his family and intense struggle with sin that he developed a deep need for God and learned to depend on God's grace in his life.

I used to always wonder what caused otherwise healthy police families to fall into patterns of dysfunction. I believe there is a common thread between our heroes of scripture and our own stories. I believe there is an important truth that every lawman and soldier should take away from our biblical heroes' hardships and brokenness. Our call to represent a godly image of service, sacrifice, and righteousness in our families should always precede our service, sacrifice, and standard of righteousness we are called to serve in our communities and nation.

In my experience, officers who experience ongoing family

difficulties and turmoil usually have fallen into the unhealthy pattern of failing to give their families the same level of dedicated and faithful service as they do their jobs. In fact, we can become so inundated with the work of law enforcement that many times if we're not careful, our families will begin to feel like suspects. A large part of the work demands that we interpret and enforce laws. I really believe this aspect of our work hardens our hearts and breeds attitudes of cynicism and arrogance that most spouses and children find difficult to understand and deal with. We become experts at showing others the God of justice. Rarely does the culture promote or lend itself to projecting the God of mercy. Unfortunately, sometimes, this can become a truth in our homes. We spend so much time with our hearts rooted in "law," our hearts can become incapable of extending "grace" where it should always be present . . . in our homes. For it is in a heart rooted in grace that our families will find the love and support they need to be whole.

Considering the unbelievable sacrifices that officers and soldiers make daily to protect us, they deserve to have healthy and blessed families. I can assure you that God is well aware of our sacrifices, hurts, and pain, and he desires very deeply for us to not have to walk around feeling like aliens in a foreign land.

I want to note that there are tons of healthy and happy law enforcement families. As I have observed them and their interactions over the years, there is always one consistent and glaring quality: a presence of humility in the officer. These officers and servicemen are not only sacrificial in their posture toward their jobs, they are always gracious and humble servants to their families. Their families are always their top priorities. I hear officers say all the time that their families come first, but so many times their actions tell a different story. Living sacrificially toward our families is more than providing for our families and working secondary or side jobs to pay for vacations or private schools. Those things are noble, and our families deserve them; however, how we walk before them and our attitudes toward them is what they will remember most. Therefore, it is the officer or soldier who is willing to live circumspectly and humbly before our God who positions their family to sidestep the dysfunctional trap that ensnarled some of our heroes of faith and can so easily ensnarl us all. The Lord shows us very clearly and practically how our families can be blessed from top to bottom.

Let's look at Psalm 128:1–4 for a moment. It says:

"Blessed is everyone who fears the Lord, who walks in his ways! You shall eat the fruit of the labor of your hands; you shall be blessed, and it shall be well with you. Your wife will be like a fruitful vine within your house; your children will be like olive shoots round your table. Behold, thus shall the man be blessed who fears the Lord."

As we look at the above text through a law enforcement lens, in relation to the full character of God as revealed through the biblical story line, we can say, then, that *blessed is the law enforcement officer who loves, recognizes, and acknowledges all God has done for him/her and therefore is compelled to model what it means to live upright before God in service to his/her family.* God purposely extends the lawman who loves him the blessings of his providential care and divine favor. When asked by others how he's doing, the officer shall be able to answer most assuredly, "All is well," and mean it. If married, the wife will be the supermom she was destined to be. She shall manage her household with divine precision and bring out the best in her family. Their children, having witnessed the godly model and standard of healthy family dynamics lived out before them, eventually become respectful, responsible, and productive, bearing the same fruit of righteousness in their own lives.

With God's help, my family and I have healed a great deal, but we still have a lot of healing to do. My wife and I survived some rough years by God's grace. I often think about why she stayed with me in the early years, but then she told me one day that she always believed that God would heal our land. She was right.

CHAPTER 4

The Call to Serve the Community

While walking by the Sea of Galilee, he saw two brothers, Simon (who is called Peter) and Andrew his brother, casting a net into the sea, for they were fishermen. And he said to them, "Follow me, and I will make you fishers of men." Immediately they left their nets and followed him (Matthew 4:18–20 ESV).

I really believe that one of the most powerful things that can ever happen to anyone is to discover their true identity and find meaningful and sustained purpose in their chosen vocation. It's life-changing as you really begin to understand that you are not a rebel without a cause. It's liberating to realize that you have intimate and personal value to God and the assignment he has called you to matters. Sadly, most people live their whole lives without understanding the depth of God's love for them and how so much of what we do in service to him, he uses to bless the people we are called to.

The call to law enforcement is an uncommon calling, to say the least. It's a call that even today I'm glad I accepted and fulfilled. We know that the call to law enforcement is not without its challenges. We know this all too well; however, it is the most exciting, fun, and rewarding career, in spite of any inherent dangers and uncertainty.

I became a Christian after I had been on the force for about 12 years and temporarily considered leaving due mostly to a serious misinterpretation of the Bible. I didn't know the God of justice and mercy at that time and thought my duties as a police officer was in serious conflict with my faith. Boy, was I wrong! One day while in my "Story of Christianity" class in seminary, we discussed a man named William Wilberforce. There is a quote by Wilberforce that stuck with me. He said, "My walk is a public one. My business is in the world, and I must mix in the assemblies of men or quit the post which providence seems to have assigned me." As we examined the life of Wilberforce, I was fascinated to learn that he had a deep and intense sense of his spiritual calling, which led to a deep sorrow and conviction at what he deemed was the wickedness of the slave trade. He ultimately felt called to a greater purpose, not in the larger church but in his community. He deemed that his spiritual calling by God was to be fulfilled in and through his secular job. I now understood that I was not only called to serve God in the church, but that I was also called to serve God in my job as a police officer. I realized that if God was calling me to serve him as a police officer, he would also teach me and equip me to do it in such a manner that was pleasing to him.

As we talk about "the call," it's important to understand that unfortunately not everyone who wears the badge has been called to law enforcement in the sense of purpose and destiny. For some, they only see it as a job with a decent amount of job security.

When was the first time you realized you wanted to be

in law enforcement? Was there any one singular incident, or was it a series of events that led to a heightened sense of awareness that you were created to be an officer? Perhaps it was a sense of patriotic duty or a deep sense of disdain for community predators. Maybe it was a feeling of wanting to live by a standard or code of honor and be a part of a brotherhood. I believe it's important to identify and carefully reflect on our calling to law enforcement for one very important reason. I believe law enforcement officers are called to law enforcement. I believe very deeply that not only are we called, we are called by God himself in that he divinely orchestrates events in our lives to get us ready to accept the call.

I can remember one night while I was in the eleventh grade, hearing a knock on the front door of our apartment. My mother was upstairs, so I walked over to the door and asked, "Who is it?" three times. I should have walked away, but my curiosity got the best of me. I opened the door . . . and suddenly I was staring down the barrel of a .38-caliber revolver. The gunman forced me back into the house and kept the gun pressed firmly against my head. He told me it was a robbery and no one would be hurt if I cooperated. His face was partially covered so I couldn't see his identity. I wasn't really afraid for my safety. I was worried about my mother. Rather than being scared as I should have been, I was angry and wanted to hurt this man in the worst way. Several times I thought about trying to disarm him. Each time I was about to go for it, something would restrain me. I couldn't really explain it at the time. He called my mother down and kept the gun to my head until she gave him what little money we had. He got his money and disappeared into the night, never to be seen again. I felt powerless and after the anger came the tears of guilt that I wasn't able to protect my mother. I decided that there was something I could do. I could dedicate my life to criminal justice and do everything in my power to ensure that I prevented as many people as possible from feeling what I felt that horrible night.

The question is, did God send him? Of course not. God is good, and that man was horribly wicked. Could God have stopped him? Of course, he could have. This may be hard for some to understand, but I believe God did allow it; however, I believe he was there protecting my mom and me the entire time. Would I have become an officer without this event happening? Perhaps, but this incident created in me a passion for justice that still burns today. Before this incident, I just wanted to be a policeman. After this incident, I wanted to be a world changer.

Prior to accepting the call to the vocation God calls us to, I believe he engages us along the way necessarily, freely, and contingently to prepare our hearts and get us positioned to accept the call as evidenced in our text.

Imagine minding your own business on your job one day, only to be tapped on the shoulder by a stranger who simply says, "Follow me!" In our text, when Andrew and Peter were approached by Jesus initially, they were already doing what they had a love and deep passion for doing, which was fishing. When we think about the sense of being called to law enforcement, we can certainly conclude, then, that we are inspired and have the itch and inclination to be police officers long before we actually receive the call and are commissioned. It's interesting that although they didn't know it, the Lord was already preparing them for a life of service to his people. When I read this text, my own limited and Westernized thinking gets the best of me because it says that they immediately dropped their nets and followed Jesus.

Contextually, it appears to have at least made some sense to them, but it still challenges me comparatively. It's hard for me to believe they totally understood what was happening when they were initially approached by Jesus. Perhaps that's just how God wanted it. Jesus could not share with them exactly what they were getting into because it would have terrified them to the point of running from their destiny.

Likewise, most police academy recruits only have a small glimpse of the magnitude of the internal and external pressures of a career spent serving under a microscope, where any wrong decision or tactical mistake is potentially the lead story on the evening news. If I had known then what I know now about the intricacies of wearing a badge, perhaps fear would have gotten the best of me and changed the course of my life. For this reason, it's good the disciples didn't know what they were really getting into, considering that nearly all but one would be called to make the ultimate sacrifice as martyrs on behalf of those they were called to serve.

When the disciples got the call, I'm sure they were uneasy, but not enough to make them say no. If you really think about it, from our own experiences, we know that whenever God steps into your story, things are never the same again. The call to Jesus is first and foremost a call to him relationally. It is rooted in Christ's Lordship in our lives, and so there is something so divinely intoxicating about being in God's presence that we are unable to resist the call to him or the subsequent call to service.

We should be encouraged in our callings, knowing that we have the full backing of heaven to help us to pursue justice well and be a beacon of light and safety for the community. Along with calling the disciples to service, Jesus also made them a promise to develop them, equip them, and prepare them to walk in their calling and divine purpose. He said intently, "I will make you a fisher of men" (v. 19). We are not called to be fishermen as they were; as lawmen, we are called to be peacemakers. We should therefore never forget that we are foundationally called to a community and that should always undergird our will to do whatever is necessary to be the peacemakers we are called to be for the citizens we are called to protect and serve.

What is really disabling about this passage and perhaps the call itself is that every lawman has to unfortunately make the decision to walk away from his previous civilian life in order to faithfully fulfill the high standard of character expected of law enforcement. When the disciples were called and chose to follow, they immediately chose to leave some people and relationships they cared about in the past. It is the same sacrifice of the call to the law enforcement community. Just like with the disciples, God calls us out of our comfort zones, the security and familiarity of our families and friends. Truth is, police work changes us and shifts our thinking. Because of the very nature of the work, so many of those early relationships before the police academy are never the same again. As I'm sure the disciples found out, every lawman discovers that there is a tremendous amount of personal life-altering sacrifice in accepting the call. Despite what is required to fulfill our calling, nothing trumps being called, gifted, and equipped by God himself to do and pursue the very thing he created and destined you to do for his glory.

Even as an adolescent, I always liked helping people. I suppose I have always had the heart of a peacemaker. God shaped me with his hands that way. If you're reading this, he probably shaped you in a similar fashion.

There's certainly a uniqueness in every call. I'm sure your call to service is quite possibly a little or even a lot different from mine, and that's okay. What's important is that you said yes and obeyed the command to drop everything and follow him.

CHAPTER **#5**

God's Special Servant

Therefore whoever resists the authorities resists what God has appointed (Romans 13:2 ESV).

I was watching the news this morning and saw a story that stirred my heart a great deal. Apparently, overnight there had been a drive-by shooting at one of the local nightclubs which ended in a pursuit by police and subsequent car crash between the fleeing suspect's car and an innocent motorist who had no idea what was happening. The innocent motorist's car was badly damaged, but thankfully, the driver only sustained a minor injury. Both suspects were caught by the officers, arrested, and taken to jail. Police recovered drugs and weapons from the suspects' vehicle and evidence of the drive-by shooting.

As I sat there in front of my television, my heart was filled with gratitude for the officers on duty that night. I thought to myself, *There's a reason why we feel safe to live our lives and go out and have fun with our friends and families.* Indeed, there is a very good reason, and I was looking at them on my television screen. The officers on duty that night and every other law enforcement officer in their respective agencies are the reason why we are able to sleep peacefully at night. It is because of their courageous sacrifices that we are able to live in relative peace.

As I sat on the edge of my bed getting a little misty-eyed as I reflected over my own career, I grabbed my Bible and began to read the 13th chapter of Romans because I suddenly felt like I needed to. As I examined verses 1–7, I had to stop and start thanking God because I realized something. When God divinely commissioned and appointed law enforcement, wrath was not on his mind. That was not his thinking at all. Love was! Compelled by his deep and intense love for the community and his heart for justice and mercy, God reveals himself through the manifested presence of law enforcement.

In and through his special law enforcement servants, God graciously and necessarily administers two forms of justice.

#1. Criminal justice (*Justice*)—A system of law enforcement and justice agencies, established by government, that seeks to deter crime and hold others accountable who break laws. An easier way to say it is to say that law enforcement and the justice system makes sure normal stays normal.

#2. Restorative justice (*Mercy*)—Focuses on crime victim justice, offender rehabilitation, and the larger community. An easy-to-understand example of restorative justice is, let's say, an offender or law violator being restored through a community service program.

Seeing police work from God's perspective links law enforcement with the very heart of God. As we partner with him, he helps us to see law enforcement work the way he sees it. He helps us to love justice and mercy. When we look down at those shiny badges on our shirts, we should remember under whose authority we exist. If God instituted us, then, that is heaven's badge that we carry each day.

Every police officer should understand the very special place he has in the eyes of God. I want to encourage you today to begin to reflect on just how important you are in the plan and purposes of God in relation to his love and good intentions for our communities. Yes, it's true; you are doing God's work. He uses you every single day to either hold someone accountable who has defied the system of justice he alone established for our good, or he uses you to be a conduit of his love and compassion to crime victims, and, in some instances, even offenders. No matter what, he cares for you and sees the best in you.

What an awesome privilege it is to be chosen by the hand of God and set apart to be a police officer. It is encouraging to know that no matter the situation, God considers us special and as his special representatives on earth, law enforcement can be certain that God almighty is always with us *every* step of the way.

An Ethical Foundation (Core Values)

"Blessed are the <u>poor in spirit,</u> for theirs is the kingdom of heaven.
"Blessed are <u>those who mourn,</u> for they shall be comforted.
"Blessed are the <u>meek,</u> for they shall inherit the earth.
"Blessed are those who hunger and <u>thirst for righteousness,</u> for they shall be satisfied.
"Blessed are the <u>merciful,</u> for they shall receive mercy.
"Blessed are the <u>pure in heart,</u> for they shall see God.
"Blessed are the <u>peacemakers,</u> for they shall be called sons of God.
"Blessed are those who are <u>persecuted for righteousness'</u> <u>sake,</u> for theirs is the kingdom of heaven.
"Blessed are you when others revile you and <u>persecute you</u> <u>and utter all kinds of evil against you falsely</u> on my account.
Rejoice and be glad, for your reward is great in heaven, for so they persecuted the prophets who were before you (Matthew 5:3–12 ESV).

What makes a great law enforcement officer or soldier? No matter who you are or where you work in law enforcement, there is always the burning question of what defines greatness in service to a nation or community. What does it look like? What is the standard that inevitably determines greatness in such a broad scope of security and crime-fighting duties and how do we achieve it?

Let me say that I have no reservation in boldly proclaiming that most officers do their job the right way and are excellent servants to the community, as they should be. However, I'm also aware that some officers are easily influenced, especially new officers, and can find themselves in the abyss of ethical confusion while trying to figure out their position in relation to the law enforcement culture as a whole and depending on where assigned, their unit/platoon's normative ethical standards and practices. This is why it is so important for every officer to be firmly rooted in a solid ethical foundation to help guide and govern their actions on the job.

So what do we mean when we say ethics in law enforcement? The simplest way to define ethics is, guided by a standard of beliefs and undergirded by a set of core values, doing the right thing, all the time. So how do we determine what's right and what's wrong? We can zero in on the societal values that our hearts tell us are good, like honesty, integrity, compassion, and justice, and just accept that they are good, or we can look to the one who we know is good as a basis for establishing an ethical foundation. Without getting into a long theological explanation of what makes God good, let me just say that if we can acknowledge that he is God, then we can surely say he is good. Why? Because only something that is infinitely good can love something as rebellious and selfish as the human heart. The ethical foundation that God has provided in his Word for law enforcement is rooted in the heart of who God is and who he calls his law enforcement servants to be. Policing a community and defending a nation according to God's will and plan is ultimately our best chance at avoiding the trap of falling into our own or someone else's contaminated "stinking thinking." Ethically, it gives us our best chance to do the job the right way without having to compromise our character and integrity and shame our families and our God for making unethical choices. The badge is a symbol of public trust in its first responders. Whenever law enforcement officers violate their code of ethics, they weaken the community's trust in its officers. Greatness is not about personal accomplishments; rather, it's about humility in service to others. We should never want the community to lose faith in its respective law enforcement agency.

Perhaps this is one of the things Jesus had in mind when preparing his disciples to send into the world, when he provided them with a solid ethical foundation as reflected in the Sermon on the Mount listed above (Matthew 5:3–12). This text emphasizes the principle marks of Christian character and conduct in relation to God and to men, and the blessings which rests on those who consistently live out these principles.

We talked about the call in chapter four. It's interesting that right after Jesus called his disciples and before they were ever assigned any duties, he made sure that they had a set of core values to guide their actions. The disciples had to have surely been asking themselves, what is Jesus asking us to do in preparation to serve him? As we in the law enforcement community get up each day and put on our uniforms and prayerfully prepare our hearts for duty, this is the question that meets us and is always ever before us as protectors and servants of God's people. What is God calling us and enabling us, his ministers of justice, to be and do?

As Jesus stood on the hill overlooking his disciples, he began to lay the ethical foundation for his followers. I really believe that these principles are one of the real and tangible ways God reveals himself very personally to law enforcement. As we surrender ourselves to his Lordship, he fills us and graces us with the power to perfect these character traits in our own lives, personally and professionally. So let's view them through the lens of law enforcement.

Blessed are the poor in spirit (v. 3) Unfortunately, in law enforcement, we can be viewed as mean-spirited, arrogant, and unapproachable by some in the community. In many cases, officers can give the appearance of being judgmental and indifferent to the less fortunate. I know I spent so many years in law enforcement looking judgmentally at the brokenness of some of those I encountered on duty, yet was unaware and unwilling to consider my own condition. Whenever officers are continuously getting internal affairs complaints for verbal and/or physical abuse, a failure to adhere to an ethical standard in relation to how they relate to God and man is usually the root cause of the problem. As servants to the community, we need to always assume a posture of humility. It is the key to going home at the end of your shift unshaken and is the difference in being able to get quality rest. Trust me, it makes a real difference. Acknowledging the issues of our own hearts and recognizing our deep need for God's grace helps us in improving our attitudes in how we relate to the community . . . *for theirs is the Kingdom of heaven.*

Blessed are those who mourn (v. 4) Serving a community and defending a nation is unbelievably hard. In dealing daily with the manifested ugliness of the human condition in "real time," there will inevitably be many days that we go home brokenhearted. In the early years, I was always robotic in my approach to the job. I thought that the best way to deal with seeing so much devastation was to block it all out and to not feel. The only problem was that I wasn't able to turn it on and off. When I got home, I couldn't suddenly turn my feelings back on, and then my family relationships suffered. We are not robots; we are men and women who feel like everyone else. There is a blessing in knowing that it's healthy and okay to acknowledge that sometimes things we encounter on duty bother us. Yes, we should maintain a professional image on duty, but that does not mean that we have to always act like we have it altogether, especially when we go home to our families . . . *for they shall be comforted.*

Blessed are the meek (v. 5) Meekness can be defined as quiet strength; strength under control in how we relate to others. One of the most unsettling things that can happen in law enforcement is to calmly bring peace to a hostile situation . . . only to have another officer show up late with a poor attitude and say something to reignite or re-escalate the incident. Officers by their attitudes and strength of character always have a chance to bring a presence of peace in every situation. In handling community disturbances and conflicts, sometimes inexperienced officers usually try to impose their will on others to gain compliance, and often it ends with them having to deal with some type of aggressive or passive resistance. Officers who are gifted at resolving conflicts all exhibit gentle spirits and attitudes of self-control. One of my mentors, Sgt. Joe Myers, used to say all the time, "The day that you gain control of your emotions is the day that you grow up." Joe is one of the meekest men I know, yet is one of the strongest. He's someone I admire and respect very deeply . . . *for they shall inherit the earth.*

Blessed are those who hunger and thirst for righteousness (v. 6) We hunger and thirst for righteousness in law enforcement when nothing is more important to us than our character and integrity and doing justice well. We chase after God's heart and pursue justice in grateful response to the God who loves us, created us, and called us to be his ministers of justice. With everything in us, we try to do justice well with an eye toward pleasing God. Doing justice well means that we are sworn to hold others accountable who break our laws. Although we may have to arrest and handcuff them, we don't have to mistreat them and strip them of their dignity. As a Christian officer, rarely did I ever consider letting anyone go who broke the law. However, I always made sure that I, and later, the detectives who worked for me, always treated others with respect. Of course, there were times when we had to use force to bring some situations under control. But when those incidents are over, they're over. Once the suspect is handcuffed, it needs to most assuredly be over . . . *for they shall be satisfied.*

Blessed are the merciful (v. 7) Inevitably, in law enforcement, we will undoubtedly come in contact with people in our communities on duty who need our help. This happens several times daily for most in law enforcement. Being merciful should be easy for us since many of us became officers in the first place because we genuinely wanted to help people. To stay fortified in our calling, it requires us to have the right attitude toward people. We need to remember that the community is not there to serve us; we are there to serve *them*. Again, God calls us not only to justice but to mercy as well . . . *they shall receive mercy.*

Blessed are the pure in heart (v. 8) Being pure in heart has nothing to do with working in this most noble of vocations. It is easy to assume that because we wear a badge and uniform and because we do good works, that makes us good, but that's not necessarily true. The high suicide rate among officers tells us that is not true. Putting on a happy face but dying inside makes you a whitewashed tomb—outwardly beautiful but inwardly rotting. Trust me, I have been there, going home day after day feeling empty and turning to alcohol and food to comfort the pain of my broken heart. There is only one way that we can have a pure heart and be inwardly cleansed to do the job to the uttermost: a complete surrender to the Lordship of Jesus Christ, who calls you to himself and this noble profession . . . *for they shall see God.*

Blessed are the peacemakers (v. 9) We are defined by state statute as peace officers. That is our mandate. To restore peace to each and every situation we are called to. The meek and pure in heart are masters at being peacemakers, as they always stand ready to facilitate reconciliation between adversaries. They can calm the seas of the most difficult of situations. The easiest way to determine if we have restored peace in a given incident is whether or not officers have to return for a subsequent call. Peacemaking is where we find our ultimate purpose and fulfillment in law enforcement . . . *for they shall be called sons of God.*

Blessed are you when others revile you and persecute and utter all kinds of evil against you on my account (v. 10–11) It's interesting that Jesus transitions here from peacemaking to persecution. Anyone in law enforcement has had the unfortunate circumstance of having to deal with angry and perhaps combative people. You name it, a law enforcement officer has been called it. I will be the first to say that law enforcement has made some mistakes in their posture and attitudes toward certain communities historically. Unfortunately, some we protect and serve feel they are justified in their hostility toward law enforcement, but I would have to say God disagrees. Truth is that no matter how well we serve the community, some people in the community will always hate who we are and what we stand for. They believe justice is a one-way street. Because they have no idea what it takes to be able to do what we do every day, we should never be provoked to respond in anger to the foolishness of obnoxious verbal attacks. I think most of us learn pretty early that if you feel the need to respond each time someone talks negatively about law enforcement, you will be one miserable soul at the end of your tour of duty. In a fallen world, it's part of the work. I tried to remember that men and women before me had to endure suffering for righteousness' sake. No matter how much the people we are serving turn on us, Christ suffered more. His pain was infinitely greater than anything we could ever face. As we wear the shiny badges of justice on our uniforms, we are also handsomely adorned with badges of suffering in our hearts. It is the work to which we have been called and endure because we remember the hand that chose and called us only chooses a few to protect and serve his nation and communities . . . *rejoice and be glad for great is your reward in heaven.*

Why does it really matter to have a solid ethical foundation?

I used to discuss ethics with the narcotics detectives who worked for me all the time. I set an ethical standard and for the most part they followed, but you never really know if the seeds you have sown have fallen on good ground. Of course, I prayed for them, but I wasn't sure.

While on Facebook recently, one of the detectives who worked for me named Cunningham posted the following . . .

"Here's the unfortunate conundrum about police work. (From my point of view, at least). And I think if more officers understood and accepted it, they could sleep better at night. Doing this job, honestly and fairly means that you will always get the bad guy the best way you could. But doing this job honestly and fairly also means that sometimes you won't get the bad guy!"

When I asked him about it, he said that watching my consistent approach to ethics in law enforcement had contributed heavily to shaping his thinking about doing the job the right way.

So it matters what we model to the officers around us. What if, like Jesus, we all were willing to make disciples and provide them with a solid ethical foundation? We could do so much to heal some of the tensions between the community and its law enforcement agencies. Why is it reasonable to do this? It's simple. The people in the community are the very people who make up juries. It is imperative to the stability of our communities that the community has faith and confidence in its officers and their credibility.

I would like to end here how I began this chapter with the question, what makes a great officer or soldier? Actually, depending on who you ask, there are many schools of subjective thought regarding this tough question. One thing is for certain. If God were to offer his input as to the qualities of a great officer, strength of character would be at the top of the list.

CHAPTER **#7**

Our Assignment: The Means Streets of Jericho

A man was going down from Jerusalem to Jericho and fell among robbers, who stripped him and beat him and departed, leaving him half dead (Luke 10:30 ESV).

I talked earlier about the incident of my mom and me being robbed at gunpoint and the incredible effect it had on me while I was in high school. It made me angry, and it made me sad that it happened. Later I wrestled with fear of what could have been the end result. We could have been killed! My mom never mentioned the incident or discussed it with me, but I know it affected her deeply.

My neighborhood was a tight-knit small housing development named Laclede Town. We lived in one of the newer developments named Breakthrough West. I loved living there growing up, but looking back now, I can say from my perspective that it was a dangerous place to live in relative terms. Whenever we talk about neighborhoods being dangerous, what we really mean to say is that it's dangerous, but usually only for visitors to the neighborhood. Lots of violent incidents happened in my old neighborhood, but most of the time the victims were outsiders. That's kind of how it goes. Of course, my mom and I were exceptions to the rule.

The violence that sometimes happened in my old neighborhood wasn't that different from the neighborhood of Jericho Road found in Luke 10:25–37. The reality is that people who wander into such neighborhoods can become victims of crimes. The mean streets of Jericho found in our text remind me a lot of the neighborhoods I spent years patrolling. Just like in the parable, the roads in some of our law enforcement agencies' neighborhoods regularly lead us into the paths of the victims of the most heinous of crimes, such as domestic violence, rape, robbery, assault, and often even murder.

There are several things in this story that are worth pointing out. First, let's get a clear picture. A man is traveling alone from one town to another and ends up on a dangerous road. The text indicates that as he traveled he encountered a group of "stick-up men," who not only beat him severely; they also humiliated him by stripping him of his clothing. With robbery as their clear motive, they left him on the side of the road confused and bleeding with severe trauma.

As I read the text, I made a few interesting observations. First, the text doesn't indicate if they took anything of value. We know that some people traveled by donkey during that time but the text doesn't say they stole money and/or took his donkey. As I read it through the lens of law enforcement, I believe it was an early example of a senseless crime. I believe they were probably looking for more, but since the victim didn't have anything, they settled for his clothing for their trouble. Just like in the text, sometimes in law enforcement, we respond to some robberies that leave us shaking our heads. I used to always walk away from such incidents with the same burning question: What type of person would do such a thing?

I also noticed in the text that not one but *two* clergymen saw this man lying on the side of the road, probably unconscious and lying in a pool of blood and actually crossed over to the *other* side of the road to avoid having to help this injured man. Now, we need to remember that they did things a little different in the Ancient Near East, but the whole point of telling the story was for Jesus to contrast those who pretend to take care of people and those who actually take care of people. The two clergymen were so concerned with their laws that it blocked them from loving and having compassion for people, at least in this instance.

Now we come to the heart of the matter. There is one distinct truth worth pointing out, and it is this: There are some neighborhoods and communities that are so bad that even the church is unwilling to go and help. I know there are plenty of church buildings in those neighborhoods, but in my experience of 21 years in law enforcement, rarely when these types of incidents happen have I responded and found "the church." That is not to say that the church doesn't get involved when people fall victim to crimes in the community, because they often do. There are Good Samaritans all over the world who are willing to get involved. My point is to suggest that more than anyone, the church should be partnering with law enforcement, but that's just not always the case . . . if ever.

In the story, the first responder is the Good Samaritan of the text. Without any real first responders at the time, it's who God used to tend to the wounds of the victim and get him the help he needed. As we put this story in a twenty-first-century context, I feel safe in saying that the Good Samaritan of the story is reflective of our first responders and their duties. Notice when the Samaritan first arrived, his concern was compassionate concern for the preservation of human life. That sounds like a law enforcement/first responder to me. Before we ever think about catching the person responsible for the crime, our job is to preserve human life if at all possible. This often means rendering first aid, which is the first thing the Samaritan does in the text. The next thing he did was to take him to the local inn to ensure he received extended care and had a chance to heal. Again, this sounds like the duties of first responders. It is the equivalent of taking a crime victim to the hospital for medical treatment, or a female victim of domestic violence to an abuse shelter, or a child abuse victim to foster care, or a homeless person to a homeless shelter. Yes, I'm confident in saying that law enforcement, more than anyone, is reflective of the Good Samaritan of the text.

The mean streets of Jericho are where we, as law enforcement officers, have an opportunity to make a real impact in the lives of others. Not only in compassionately meeting the needs of our victims but also in the apprehension of the suspects. The suspects on the Jericho Road have to be brought to justice, and we will use every available resource, leaving no stone unturned, to find them and bring them to justice. It is what God expects and demands of his agents of justice. It ultimately means this: In each situation we face, we need to always remember that we are the presence of God. Therefore, when we respond, we need to respond with the compassionate hearts for victims and controlled, ethical determination in catching the perpetrators.

In closing, here is a blueprint in easy-to-follow bullet points to provide a framework for God-centered policing for contemporary law enforcement on the mean streets of your agency's Jericho.

"This is what the Lord says: Administer justice and righteousness. Rescue the victim of Robbery from the hand of the oppressor (Jeremiah 22:3 ESV)."

Administer Justice . . . Enforce the laws we swore to uphold with all courage and honor.

Administer Righteousness . . . Do justice the right way with an eye toward our ethical foundation which is rooted in professionalism, character, and integrity.

Rescue Victims . . . Serve people; hold others accountable who seek to harm them.

Preserve Peace . . . The heart of who we are and what we are called by God to do. For we are preservers of peace.

CHAPTER **#8**

All Things to All People

*To the Jews I became like a Jew, to win the Jews. To those
under the law I became like one under the law, so as to win
those under the law. To those not having the law I became
like one not having the law, so as to win those not having
the law. To the weak I became weak, to win the weak. I have
become all things to all people so that by all possible means
I might save some (1 Corinthians 9:20–22 ESV).*

Recently I overheard an officer who was clearly frustrated
dealing with an ongoing situation he was facing make the
statement, "We can't be all things to all people!" I began to
think about his comments, and I concluded that what he was
probably trying to say was that as law enforcement, we can't
please everyone. I agree with the officer about not being able
to please everyone; and I don't think we should try. However,
we should pursue excellence in all that we do as we serve the
public. After all, isn't that the work we are called to do?

So what does it mean to be all things to all people in a
law enforcement context? What does that look like? I believe
it means that in any given instance or situation, we should

meet people in the midst of their personal trauma or crisis. We should be willing to adapt to their situation by responding with the necessary resources to meet their emergency or need. We should try to deal compassionately and empathetically with them, remembering that at some juncture in our lives we have been them, could have been them, and still could make a life-altering decision or mistake and end up like them. I don't know about you, but that humbles me. Being all things to all people, then, reflects law enforcement officers who have hearts for restoring peace to each and every situation we face. Listen, as I have already stated, there is a certain element of our customers who are never going to accept who we are and what we do. I don't believe that should matter to us one bit regarding who they are, what they say, or how they may feel about us personally. It's not who they are that's important, for we are always blessed with opportunities every day to show the community the essence of who we are . . . Peace Officers.

I can remember one brutally hot and humid summer day, my partner and I responded to a call for a large disturbance. When we arrived, there was a large crowd arguing and shouting obscenities at each other. Thankfully, our presence and professional image was enough to calm and disburse most of the angry crowd. As is usually the case, however, there is always a remnant that remains and seems unrelenting in their determination to wreak havoc and provoke others, especially law enforcement, into verbal and/or physical confrontations.

On this particular day, there was one young lady who just wouldn't let up and began to say some things to my partner that no officer should ever have to endure from the public. She was clever and successful in her provocation of my partner. I could clearly see he was as angry as I had ever seen him.

The woman had broken the law and was subsequently arrested for the crime of peace disturbance. As I was handcuffing her, my partner said something offensive and degrading to her that he should not have said. Perhaps some would view it as a racial slur, but I knew the officer quite well, and I never viewed it in that manner at all. However, I was deeply concerned about what had just happened. While I didn't agree or like what he said, in that moment, in that instance, being all things to all people meant that I needed to be his partner. That was not the time to abandon or get angry at him. At that moment, I remembered that I had said things plenty of times I wish I could take back. I knew what he said was something we would have to deal with privately as partners (and we did), but in that moment, although I hated what he said, my partner needed me to be his partner, and I was.

To the young man on our beat who gets into trouble as a juvenile, we become juveniles again, remembering that we all made some poor choices as adolescents.

To the high school student who is being victimized by a bully, we become victims, remembering that there have been times in our lives when perhaps we were bullied and what that felt like. It's not easy to go to school or work in fear.

To the new officer in your agency, we become rookies again, remembering the trembling and trepidation of walking into the station on the first day for duty and what it was like not to know anyone.

To the criminal, we can even be all things to him/her. As with any criminal we encounter, we should stand ready to meet any resistance with the necessary force. We can absolutely find balance here without losing our edge. We can speak to him/her in terms that he/she understands. We can choose not to judge him/her. This is not some new strategy.

The best officers, those who have an abundance of informants, understand this principle and apply it in every encounter with suspects.

Take a look back over your career and you will quickly realize what makes us different from every other profession. What grants us our privileged status as God's ambassadors of justice? What sets us apart (not above) from the community we serve is the fact that we really are all things to all people. Isn't that what makes us law enforcement? No other profession possesses our unique skill set. We truly are all things to the community. Over the course of our careers, in responding to regular calls for service as well as conducting investigations and routine patrol, we have all had to be or will have to be medics, lawyers, counselors, priests, babysitters, mechanics, psychiatrists, teachers, coaches, taxi drivers, organizers, administrators, and the list goes on and on. I'd say that makes us all things to all people. Wouldn't you?

CHAPTER **#9**

Sometimes We Need to Withdraw

*But now even more the report about him went abroad, and
great crowds gathered to hear him and to be healed of their
infirmities. But he would withdraw to desolate places and
pray (Luke 5:15–16 ESV).*

Have you ever reported for duty carrying what seemed
like the world on your shoulders, or have you ever spent an
entire shift dealing with the problems of others, and arrived
home, realizing that you were depleted and had nothing left
for your family? I'm sure you have, and I want you to be encouraged because you're in very good company. Whether
dealing with the death of a loved one, family dynamics or
heath issues, or perhaps the weightiness of an Internal Affairs
Complaint, which are rarely totally baseless, the reality is . . .
Sometimes life inevitably happens, and sometimes it can be
overwhelming.

Truth is, when we put on that uniform every day and report for duty, we are expected to show up ready to serve the
community in a professional manner, in spite of what we may
be going through personally. When we get home at the end

of our shifts, our friends and family deserve our absolute best. Unfortunately, it's not always that easy.

So what do you do when you are emotionally depleted and you don't have anything left for anyone? You know, those times when you are cynical, irritable, and snappy. As I see it, we can do a couple of things to remedy the situation. We can put on a superficial happy face and suffer in silence as we engage our family, friends, and the community at work, or we can actually adopt some strategies to help us to ensure we don't end up wounding our loved ones. You know it's funny, people may not say anything, but they can always tell when something is not quite right with us. I know I can.

Brothers and sisters, it's important that we realize that God is Superman and we are not. We are not invincible, and it's actually okay that we are not. Truth is, we are actually pretty fragile and can break easily if we are not careful.

There are some proven psychological and physiological benefits to occasionally spending 5 to 10 minutes alone in a quiet place to relax, meditate, and pray. Some of the benefits include increased happiness and emotional stability.

Sometimes Jesus would withdraw to a quiet place and pray all night. He enjoyed spending time with his Father that much. Now, I'm not suggesting you should pray all night long. It takes faith to sit alone and talk to God. If I had to say one noticeable benefit of prayer, although there are many, I would simply say this: "Prayer strengthens us where we are weak."

As it relates to the law enforcement community, I want to give you three very good reasons why sometimes we need to occasionally withdraw to a quiet place and pray.

#1. *Sometimes we need to withdraw to pray because while you may have boundaries, the people we are serving often do not (Luke 4:42)*. How many times have you been on duty sitting in a restaurant, in uniform, trying to get a quick bite to eat, only to be approached by a citizen for directions and/or legal advice, or been flagged down by a citizen while on patrol? The reality is that because of our expertise and skill set, we don't have to wait to be dispatched to problems; they will inevitably find you. Let's be honest. We have all had situations where we were somewhere handling an incident and suddenly an unrelated fight breaks out on the same street. I'm laughing as I write this, but sometimes people treat us like we are aliens; however, spending any amount of time in law enforcement will make you sometimes wonder if some of the people we are serving are from another planet. Finding time to occasionally pull away to pray will help us to handle those situations in a manner consistent with the community expectations of a law enforcement officer.

#2. Sometimes we need to withdraw to pray to successfully fulfill our calling to the community (Luke 4:43). Just like in our text, Jesus' giftedness and skill set made him quite popular in the community. People were always pulling on him, expecting him to meet their needs. While he came for this purpose, at times it took its toll on him. So, occasionally, he would withdraw to a quiet and undisturbed place to reconnect to God, his power source. Jesus knew that being a peacemaker and problem solver can drain you physically and mentally. He shows us that sneaking to a quiet place for 5 minutes to pray or sit quietly will help you to be a more centered and focused law enforcement servant and therefore be able to stay consistent in professional service to the community.

Let me ask you a question. How do you deal with anger?

How have you been taught to deal with it? There are certainly no shortages of situations that can upset us during our course of duty. For example, it's extremely upsetting to lose a case in court that you knew was airtight. When we are angered by situations on duty, we are taught to be a professional; to put it behind you and move on to the next incident. However, it's not always that easy. Unless we learn how to deal with anger, there is always the danger that our emotions can get the best of us and suddenly we have lost control on a call or at home because we didn't really know what to do with our anger. There are some things that *should* upset us. There is such a thing as righteous anger. How can you not be upset when you walk into the house and see the confused and hurting face of a child who has been molested by her stepfather for 5 years? The question is what we do with that anger? The scripture tells us to "be angry but do not sin" (Ephesians 4:26). There is something we can do with that anger and frustration, which leads us to point number three . . .

#3. Sometimes we need to withdraw because we are called to and need to pray (Luke 4:16; 1 Chronicles 16:11).

God loves you and wants to spend time with you. When we pull away to a quiet place, we find God there waiting for us. I have witnessed God doing some glorious things lately for me when I have sat before him with a troubled heart. It is in that place where things will begin to make sense and we will find comfort, courage, peace, strength, and the will to continue to serve professionally and faithfully.

CHAPTER 10

A Perfect Balance

Cornelius, a law enforcement officer, a devout man who loved God with all his household, gave generously to the people and prayed to God (Acts 10:1–2 ESV).

I believe one of the real challenges for law enforcement officers is trying to find balance in our daily lives. It's a constant battle trying to find time to adequately and fairly dedicate ourselves to the things in life that are the most important to us, like our friends and family.

In the pages of scripture, there is such a man who was able to find the perfect balance in life—so much so that it positively affected every area of his life. It's an encouraging story and gives me hope that with God's help all of us can find that sense of perfect peace and harmonious balance that we are all searching for. Cornelius, a law enforcement officer, and the first gentile convert, provides us a blueprint for finding that delicate balance in our lives. God graciously illuminates the life and heart of Cornelius and shows us that perfect balance in life is attained by focusing primarily on three important principles:

1. *Cornelius was rooted in his faith.* The scripture says that Cornelius prayed continually to God. Finding balance and peace in life as a police officer is too hard to achieve without God's help. Cornelius obviously knew this and communed with God often to find peace, joy, strength, courage, and wisdom to always be able to give others his best. As we have already learned, Jesus often pulled away to pray. That's the really cool thing about prayer. It helps us to better relate to God and others. I think it's cool that you can pray anytime, anywhere. For instance, you can pray in the squad car or the roll call room. You can find a quiet place or you can be standing in a room full of people, with your eyes wide, mouth shut, and still be able to pray in your heart. How cool is that? Prayer is simply talking to God in a posture of humility and respect. He's our Father and longs to hear from us. I used to always pray this short prayer walking out of the Narcotics Undercover Office: "Lord, please keep us all safe today. Please use us in the manner you see fit tonight. Amen!" God heard my prayers every night and was faithful in keeping us safe.

2. *Cornelius was rooted in his family and close friends.* In reading the story of Cornelius in scripture, his character and leadership qualities resonate in my heart. He was the type of person I would follow. While it is evident that he was probably a great commander and leader to his troops, he balanced his life by spending quality time with both friends and family. He was a man with a heart for giving and service. He was such an inspiration to his family that the love he displayed to others caused his family to develop hearts for giving and service as well. We should always be willing to model those things we seek to develop in our children and inspire in our friends and family.

3. *Cornelius was rooted in service to the community.* Because he had such a kind and giving heart as reflected above, he was clearly born to be law enforcement. That was his calling. It was his destiny. He embraced the call to service to God and the community. God used Cornelius mightily as he (God) worked redemptively in the heart of the Apostle Peter. Cornelius was an upstanding man in the community, and God used him to transform the hearts of others, as he did with Peter, who was struggling with diversity issues at the time but overcame them with God's help (Acts 10:28).

The Bible says very definitively that Cornelius was an upright, God-fearing man. Cornelius's fear of God was reflective of his reverence and adoration for his God. It means that he allowed God to order his steps and direct his path. Cornelius was clearly a man who was more concerned with his character and integrity than making a name for himself. Finding that perfect balance ultimately caused his name to be great. He didn't have to cut corners or break rules to get there. God exalted him into greatness. God wants to do the same for you!

CHAPTER **#11**

The Neutrality of Law Enforcement

*The soldiers planned to kill the prisoners to prevent any
of them from swimming away and escaping, but
the police commander wanted to spare Paul's life and kept
them from carrying out their plan (Acts 27:42–43 ESV).*

There is, without question, neutrality that is required of every law enforcement officer. We are called to make very difficult decisions, at a moment's notice, without the benefit of having all the "real-time facts." Still, the essence of our foundational principles requires us to be professional, fair, and impartial in each situation we face. However, let's be honest. While I would like to believe the law enforcement community executes this perfectly, the reality is, it's pretty difficult in certain situations to not be informed and influenced by previously held beliefs and assumptions. No matter if they are issues relating to race, gender, ethnicity, religious affiliation, or a political party, we take our worldview and corresponding natural character traits into each situation with us. It is unavoidable in some instances. Police policy, procedure, and protocol are designed to mitigate these factors and

THE NEUTRALITY OF LAW ENFORCEMENT (ACT 27:42-43) ➤

provide our citizens with uniformity and consistency from its police force. However, in any given incident, there can be extenuating circumstances that, in many instances, may be larger than, and may negate, policy. In some incidents, it's possible that there may not be a documented precedent and procedure for handling the incident correctly. Some incidents are so dynamic that we can hardly call them routine. They require us to make informed decisions based on our experience and, hopefully, hearts of fairness and neutrality.

In the above-captioned text of scripture, one such incident happened. The Apostle Paul, who was Jewish and a Roman citizen, had been arrested by Roman officers for preaching the Gospel which some people violently rejected. The first Christians lived in a world that didn't believe Jesus was the Messiah or the Son of God, sent from heaven to redeem and save us from our sins. Besides, Roman society had their own gods, and they were intimidated by Paul's message of being saved by grace through faith in Jesus Christ. Paul was an enemy of the state! He and some other prisoners were being transported to Rome to stand trial and to appeal to Caesar's higher court in Paul's case. Paul, previously thought to be a gentile, now invoked his Roman citizenship as a Jewish man. This allowed him to appeal his case to Caesar himself.

In a series of events, Paul had an encounter with a law enforcement commander named Julius, who, in spite of their obvious conflicting positions, chose to be fair and impartial in his encounter with Paul. The text points out that prior to beginning their voyage to Rome, Julius, in kindness to Paul, allowed him to go to his friends so they might provide for his needs (Acts 27:3). This is the essence of grace-centered law enforcement. We have all been gracious in our dealings with prisoners and may not have realized it. I guess it's the equivalent to giving a prisoner a phone call, or allowing him/ her to hug a spouse or children before going to jail. Our job is to arrest people who break the law, collect the evidence, and present our cases to the state for prosecution. Again, we do not have to look down on or mistreat prisoners just because they are under arrest. Julius could have chosen to be nasty to Paul. He could have judged him, called him names, or even beat him during their encounter. Certainly, in this instance, contextually, no one would have complained. No, Julius exemplified and modeled real professionalism in front of his men and modeled God's justice and mercy to Paul.

Prior to traveling to Rome, the Roman officials had ignored Paul's warning of sailing at that time and ran into a violent storm. Due to circumstances beyond their control, the ship's crew had to jettison overboard some of their cargo which contained the prisoners' food. After about 14 days at sea in a violent and dangerous storm, with no food, I can imagine tensions were pretty high for the officers, crew, and prisoners alike. I'm a navy veteran and have been at sea during storms and rough seas, and trust me, this was an unbelievably difficult voyage with a potentially hostile situation brewing. The scripture puts it this way . . .

Now when it was day, they did not recognize the land, but they noticed a bay with a beach, on which they planned if possible to run the ship ashore. So they cast off the anchors and left them in the sea, at the same time loosening the ropes that tied the rudders. Then hoisting the foresail to the wind they made for the beach. But striking a reef, they ran the vessel aground. The bow stuck and remained immovable, and the stern was being broken up by the surf. The soldiers' plan was to kill the prisoners, lest any should swim away and escape. But the commander, wishing to save Paul, kept them from carrying out their plan. He ordered those who could swim to jump overboard first and make for the land, and the rest on planks or on pieces of the ship. And so it was that all were brought safely to land (Acts 27:39–44, ESV).

In light of this chain of events and great biblical narrative, I would like to highlight four main points worth further reflection and consideration.

Inevitably in law enforcement we will have to make split-second choices and decisions that will negatively or positively impact our lives and the lives of others forever. This should always guide us ethically.

Although many of our incidents will often be cleared by arrest, sometimes police policy doesn't account for the totality of a specific situation. There are often God-ordained situations that have extenuating circumstances, and we must exercise discretion to handle these situations appropriately.

Although it is in many ways counter to the law enforcement culture, we have to assume a posture of loving and serving people as much as we love being police and pursuing justice. They should go hand in hand.

Trust God and allow him to partner with you each day. This will always guarantee a successful conclusion to each incident we face.

CHAPTER **#12**

The Folly of Law Enforcement

And when they had crucified him the police officers divided
his garments by casting lots. Then [the officers] sat down and
kept watch over him there (Matthew 27:35–36, ESV).

Ah, the "war stories" and "cop tales." Most of us have
heard some pretty good ones over the years. Over the course
of our careers, we will undoubtedly hear some of legendary
status.

It's probably safe to say that it's virtually impossible to
work in law enforcement for any number of years without
being the main character in a few "war stories" yourself. I can
think of a few from the Housing Unit I worked in for a couple
of years that make me laugh uncontrollably whenever I think
about them.

Folly can be described as plain old everyday foolishness.
When I think about the folly of law enforcement, I think about
some of the "war stories" I've heard over the years. I have
learned that most of the "cop tales" and "war stories" were
probably not that funny as the initial incidents were happening. In fact, I think one of the qualities of a good "war story"

or "cop tale" is there has to be a corresponding combination of shock and awe and folly attached to it. In other words, all things being equal, most reasonable people would find the incident and actions of those involved to be foolish.

There is one such incident in the pages of scripture that epitomizes the folly of law enforcement. In this incident, a very popular local celebrity receives the death penalty by crucifixion and is tasked with carrying his cross to its resting place on Calvary. I'm sure the officers on duty that day probably perceived the incident as another routine assignment based on their limited information at the time. In spite of the heinous nature of certain incidents, as far as law enforcement culture is concerned, these incidents become very routine to us. The officers on duty that day would have had no way of knowing that this local celebrity was actually God incarnate in the person of Jesus Christ, who was about to sacrifice his life to fix what was broken in the world. They knew of his claims and even mocked him for them, but we certainly can't blame the officers for not believing, especially considering the followers of Jesus didn't even really believe at the time.

At any rate, the scripture tells us that the officers engaged in a dice game to determine how the clothing of the Jesus was going to be divided between them. Wow! Talk about war stories. *"Hey, guys, remember when Officers John and Doe gambled for the clothes of that guy Jesus who claimed he was God?"* The roll call room erupts in laughter!

Before we judge those officers or any officer for their involvement in any incident of folly, perhaps we need to consider a few points for further reflection.

Incidents that lead to "war stories" are never meant to promote laughter at the expense of others. The best way to see them is the lighter side of law enforcement. Officers never set out to create "war stories" and "cop tales." They inevitably just "happen." As in the story above, although foolish, sometimes officers have quirky ways of dealing with real or perceived traumatic situations and circumstances.

As far as telling "war stories," I have learned that "war stories" actually help us to make sense out of our dangerous and often uncertain existence, that, at times, leaves officers wrestling with anxiety and fear. I believe "war stories" and "cop tales" can help to facilitate camaraderie and promote healing through laughter.

Folly or no folly, there is a part of this story that still needs to be told. The local celebrity, who proved to be the God he claimed to be, even as he hung there, suffering in silence, was well aware of the dice game of shame going on nearby for his clothing. He had every reason to be bitter and resentful at the officers, but even before they actually began to gamble for his clothing, Jesus asked the Father in heaven to forgive them, because they didn't understand what they were doing (Luke 23:34). Wow! Hopefully you are beginning to get a sense of the immense love of God for you and the grace and mercy that is always available to the law enforcement community.

I just want to encourage you today that God understands the quirky ways of the law enforcement community and the mechanisms of folly we sometimes use to help us to cope with the many difficult situations we face. In his ongoing heavenly ministry, I want you to know that Jesus continues to pray and intercede for you (Hebrews 7:25). My prayer is that you would acknowledge and believe in him and thank him by faith for continuing to take care of us, his ambassadors of justice.

CHAPTER 13

Seasons of Change

He has made everything beautiful in its time
(Ecclesiastes 3:11ESV).

One of the ways that God uses to exercise his sovereignty over creation is the timing in which he allows certain events in our lives to unfold. It often leaves us questioning God's timing and can, at times, leave us frustrated, anxious, and scratching our heads at why we experience seasons of discomfort in our lives.

Life itself for the lawman can be challenging in so many ways, especially in dealing with the rigors of trying to live a balanced life and managing the smorgasbord of emotions we have to wrestle with doing the job.

Law enforcement officers have very real problems just like everyone else and some often feel like there is no hope. I know this is true firsthand. It wasn't necessary for me to do an Internet search for statistics because for 20 years I knew every officer in my agency who committed suicide and each one devastated me. Truth is, some officers feel isolated and for a number of reasons, choose to suffer in silence.

There were many times over my career when I looked to heaven and questioned God's timing in many things going on in my life. I was hurting for one reason or another; sometimes very deeply, and I wanted God to intervene during those moments to relieve the pain and heartache. I learned that there are seasons of heartache and tears just as there are seasons of happiness and laughter. There are seasons when everything seems to be perfect, and there are seasons when nothing seems to go the way we expected. There are seasons of triumph and seasons of disappointment. Seasons change in nature and in life and are part of life's journey. God never promised that the journey would be easy, but he did promise to be an ever-present help during times of trouble (Psalm 46:1). I can tell you that God's timing is perfect, for while we were still weak, at just the right time Jesus Christ died for us (Romans 5:6). I have learned that God is really faithful if we are willing to submit our hearts to him for guidance.

Ultimately, we must remember that God created us in his image and likeness and loves us in ways my pen can't articulate. The seasons of change in our lives are always about God doing his best to help draw us closer to him, trust him, and live lives that are rooted in peace, service, justice, and a love for all of mankind.

Often, this means allowing seasons of discomfort to change our hearts from being self-centered to God-centered. How much, as a parent, would you be willing to allow your child to endure negative behavior, knowing that his or her current behavior would most certainly lead them to a lifetime of heartache? Would you be willing to lovingly watch them experience a little discomfort now to change a behavior so that they can prosper in their family relationships and on the job in the future? I feel as parents we always want what's best for our children and are willing to do whatever it takes to cultivate loving relationships with them and develop great character in them. God is no different than us parents. He's willing to allow seasons of heartache to enable us to live victoriously over the long haul. Our perspective is often to look to tomorrow, while God's perspective is slightly different. God is always concerned with our eternal destinies. He is always considering the "big" picture. God wants to make us better people for the benefit of those around us. Some seasons of change are meant to do just this. Sometimes God wants to teach us to forgive and be less judgmental, less self-centered, or even more caring toward coworkers, our families, and the community. Other times (and this is a big one), he seeks to humble us because he delights in childlike humility. As far as law enforcement officers are concerned, and as I've stated repeatedly, I know that God loves justice and established it to be carried out in the just and righteous manner he ordained. Sometimes seasons of change are meant to change behaviors that will ultimately tarnish the badge and/or bring shame on our families and discredit to our agencies.

In the end, change is often hard to accept, however so necessary for God to develop us into what he ultimately wants us to be for his glory. There will undoubtedly be seasons of change in our lives. To everything there is a season, a time for every purpose under heaven (Ecclesiastes 3:1). Purpose in your heart to embrace the seasons of change, knowing that God is developing you into an eternal masterpiece.

CHAPTER 14

Help, Hope, and Healing (The effects of policing)

While he was still speaking, there came a crowd, and the man called Judas, one of the twelve, was leading them. He drew near to Jesus to kiss him, but Jesus said to him, "Judas, would you betray the Son of Man with a kiss?" And when those who were around him saw what would follow, they said, "Lord, shall we strike with the sword?" And one of them struck the servant [police officer/soldier] of the high priest and cut off his right ear. But Jesus said, "No more of this!" And he touched his ear and healed him (Luke 22:47–51).

Have you ever been assaulted or injured while trying to make an arrest or bring someone to justice? Perhaps you have been critically wounded or lost a limb while trying to do the challenging and trying job you are called and paid to do. Maybe you were forced to use deadly force to protect human life or have witnessed or been involved in some other type of violent encounter where you are suffering from diagnosed or undiagnosed post traumatic stress disorder. Still others have had to suffer through losing a loved one, close coworker, or partner. Whatever the situation, for first responders and the law enforcement community, our reality is this: Sometimes the cost for doing justice well has a severe price. Although we count it an honor to lay it on the line every day for God's people, and although we try not to complain, sometimes, like the character Humpty Dumpty of nursery rhyme fame, we fall down and need to be put back together again. Unfortunately for Humpty Dumpty, the king and his men couldn't put him back together again. Last I heard, he went through several marriages and lived out his days as a functioning alcoholic, addicted to pain killers. Because he was unable to receive help from the king for his issues, he abused all of his wives, alienated his children, and died alone of a broken heart. Fortunately for the law enforcement community, there is a great and powerful King, whose redemptive, reconciling, and healing power is limitless, who can not only put us back together again, but he wants to and he does.

This chapter is perhaps the most personal to me because of what my personal pain and scars afford me to personally bear witness to . . . the depth of God's love for mankind and the special place in his heart for the law enforcement community. As I said before, so many of us go home every day broken, battered, and bruised from the residual effects of not just our physical but emotional duty battle scars. If we are willing to be honest and take inventory of our hearts, I know very personally that God is able to penetrate and permeate the innermost of our being and put us back together again. His deep and intimate desire to heal our physical bodies and ailing hearts is real. We are his warriors of justice, and the reality is, when we feel better, we serve people better.

Perhaps this is what Jesus had in mind when he performed

the miracle in the life of Officer Malchus (John 18:10). We have already discussed in an earlier chapter the arrest of Jesus and his gracious ways with his law enforcement servants; however, even as I read this passage right now, I cannot contain myself. I'm hopeful you can sense my excitement for what is about to happen as we come to the end of the story. Here we have Jesus who is on his way to Calvary to fulfill his destiny to die for the sins of the world. The fate of humankind is at stake, and it is all resting on his divine shoulders. Any distraction, no matter how small or minute, could disrupt him from accomplishing his goal of fixing what Adam broke in the Garden of Eden. His whole program is to deal with this sin problem once and for all and to restore and reconcile us to peace with God. It would be easy to conclude that Jesus probably had a lot on his mind, but that's just it. His interactions with each of us is real and personal as we are about to see. As the officers move in to arrest Jesus, we need to be aware that Satan always tries to have his say in the story. Jesus is not caught off guard. He knows exactly what is happening. One of the Lord's disciples, the great Apostle Peter, the first pope of the Catholic church and bishop to Rome, takes matters into his own hands. (Just as a side note, it's interesting that God would later use Peter to deal with the always relevant issue of submitting to state and federal authority; see 1 Peter 13–17). It is fascinating the tough situations that God is willing to allow us to go through to prepare us to be able to help others later.

Armed with a sword, Peter assaulted one of the arresting officers by cutting off his right ear. Okay, let's pause for a moment and really think about what just happened here through the lens of law enforcement in a contemporary context. If you would, just for a moment, please close your eyes and immerse yourself in this story and visualize what's happening here. The officers who are doing the job they are sworn to do are immediately faced with a deadly force situation. There is the immediate issue of making what we today would call a "high-profile arrest." Now the officers also have to deal with the issue of what to do with Peter, who has broken at least three pretty common contemporary laws: #1 Interfering with an arrest, #2 Assault 1st degree on an officer, and #3 Armed criminal action. Think about the magnitude of such an event from a contemporary standpoint. There's a good chance that at least one media source would have been present, not to mention all of the smartphone images that would have been taken of the incident by interested observers and later posted on Facebook, Twitter, and every other social media outlet. The arresting officers, in spite of their experience and training, had to make a split-second decision that would be critiqued throughout all human history.

Clearly, Jesus is in control of this situation but just stop and think for a moment. If you're not a soldier or officer reading this story, how would *you* have responded to such a situation? The officers responded the way officers should respond, at least in this instance, by exercising enormous restraint in this most tragic of situations. In no way am I implying that these officers did everything right in their encounters with Jesus. Scripture bears witness to the fact that they made a lot of mistakes in their treatment of Jesus. Also, in previous chapters, we dealt with the issue of law enforcement ethics. What's important to realize here in this incident is that they didn't go after Peter, although they would have been justified to use deadly force against him. Officers are always allowed by state statute to use deadly force in defense of their lives or the lives of others. Think about it! A law enforcement brother or sister with whom you've gone through the academy, sweat blood with and trained and served with, whom you love, suddenly gets attacked and seriously injured! How would *you* have responded?

One of the reasons Jesus stepped in immediately was to protect Peter, but I'm convinced that's not the only reason. Unlike Peter, Jesus was in total control of his emotions. He could have decided not even to bother with the immediacy of Peter's actions or the injured officer who, by the way, was about to take him to jail. Think about that for a second. Quite frankly, we could easily say that Jesus had bigger fish to fry at the time, right? Wrong! Nothing could be further from the truth. In spite of the enormity of what was ahead of him and considering the events leading to and on Calvary (along with the Resurrection)—these are the most important events in the history of the Christendom and, in many respects, the world—I think we would all understand if Jesus had made the decision to move closer toward the business at hand. However, that's just it . . . Healing the hurting and brokenhearted *is* the business at hand. That's why he came! In that Jesus himself ordained the authorities to be keepers of peace, he more than any other knows the daily obstacles and the effects that officers must overcome to protect and serve the community. It is evident that Peter and most people who attack officers for trying to do their jobs never stop to consider that the officer or soldier perhaps has a family at home that loves him. They never stop to consider that this lawman is not a robot of the state but a real human being who bleeds and suffers the same hurts and wrestles with the same emotions as everyone else. It would be easy to say, well, during that time, officers were killed and wounded in battle all the time. It was part of their job. We accept it as part of the job and always stand ready to lay down our lives without hesitation for the community and each other. However, that does not mean that we want to be killed or like being assaulted and injured.

Jesus takes it on his own divine shoulders to deal with this difficult and heinous issue. Jesus understood that these officers had a job to do, just as he had a job to finish. He himself initiated their authority, and he himself respected it. This incident became very personal for him. Peter did not just assault a uniform. No, this officer had a name which personalizes it for me as well. After witnessing Peter's actions, Jesus said emphatically, "No more of this!" Of course, we know that Jesus wanted Peter to know that he had to endure this cup of suffering for our sake, although Peter clearly did not understand at the time. I also believe Jesus' powerful words . . . "No more of this!" rings true today. Whenever someone attacks one of God's servants of justice, the words still are perpetually true. They still ring out today. The God of justice, God incarnate in the person of Jesus Christ still shouts at the top of his lungs to anyone who seeks to harm law enforcement: "No more of this!"

Whenever these types of incidents happen to law enforcement, there is always a cost. Police officers are experts at what I call the "Fig leaf syndrome." We become well versed in covering up. Heck, it's part of the culture. Still, being shot at and having to fight every day just to make what used to be routine arrests, being forced to chase bad guys several times a shift, witnessing the fear and pain in the eyes of victims of rape, child abuse, and domestic violence, smelling the stench of death, witnessing homelessness and helplessness daily, eventually is sure to cause some emotional battle scars that we at some point have to deal with. Unfortunately, our emotions will likely deal with us before we are ever willing to deal with them. Inwardly assessing is just not something we like to do.

In my own personal experience and professional experience of observing first responders and soldiers, there are several negative emotions that can become problematic for our heroes behind the badge because of the stress of the work. Although I didn't really recognize it at the time, I struggled with guilt, insecurity, anxiety, anger, fear, and pride. I lived in constant fear and trepidation of wondering if today was going to be the day that I would have to make the ultimate sacrifice. My heart became very judgmental and agitated sometimes at the people I was supposed to be protecting and serving. Honestly, I treated some of them like I was better than them and that later led to guilt and shame. I feel like the list can vary from person to person, depending on the law enforcement context.

Please don't get me wrong, most of what we do is quite fulfilling and a lot of fun. Chasing and arresting bad guys is so much fun for most of law enforcement; however, there are parts of the job that negatively affect us daily, stirring a wide range of negative emotions, that, if not checked, can cause a downward spiral. The downward spiral usually leads to coping mechanisms such as overindulgence in eating and excessive alcohol drinking. Since most of us are so good at hiding our ailing hearts, our supervisors and coworkers almost never know but families usually are aware that we are struggling.

We need to always remember that God loves us very deeply and intimately and wants to heal us so that we can serve to the fullest. His healing touch is available to us through law enforcement chaplains, your agency's personal assistance counselors, doctors, and/or professional therapists. God is unlimited in his resources to help you in the process of healing.

Just as he knew the name of Officer Malchus in the story previously mentioned, I want you to know that he knows *your* name and knows all about you. For some, your commanding officer may not know your name. For them, you may just be a name on the roll, but the God of all creation knows you by name. How cool is that?

CHAPTER 15

Great Faith, Great Challenges, Great Blessings

*"When Jesus heard these things, he marveled at the soldier
and turning to the crowd that followed the commander, said
I tell you, not even in Israel have I found such faith"
(Luke 7:9 ESV).*

I really believe that there are many law enforcement officers who struggle in their faith and some struggle with doubt or unbelief altogether. For the most part, we normally get to see people at their worst. Sometimes when people are at their worst, unfortunately, that can bring out the worst in us. Some are struggling with a sense of unworthiness to ask God for help due to the sometimes violent and unpopular nature of their work. Some are convinced that if there is a God, he doesn't care about us or them at all. After all, if God loves us so much, then, why is there so much crime, said the skeptical officer in his heart. Well, it would take another full chapter to try to fully answer that question; however, the short answer is this: there is crime in the world because there is sin in the world. I would add this, that God really does love you. So much so that he sent his one and only son, who was completely innocent, to die to eradicate sin's death grip over your life. When he died for us, he really conquered the sin problem once and for all. Those who choose to believe in him shall not perish but have everlasting life (John 3:16).

As we wrap up this book, I believe we have saved the best for last. I want to both encourage and remind officers of Jesus and our freedom to approach him by faith with our petitions and requests for help. We have spent a great deal of time in this book prayerfully trying to get the law enforcement community to see their inherent value to God's gracious kingdom and the many communities it entails. I'm forever prayerful that law enforcement officers will learn to trust and believe in God's miracle-working power and providence to advance his Kingdom in the law enforcement community and beyond.

Imagine being on duty one day and pulling over a vehicle for speeding. As you approach the driver's door of the vehicle and look inside, you notice a man sitting in the driver's seat wearing a white priestly collar and apparel. Would you write him a ticket? Most officers would probably say "no," but why not? Is it because somehow letting the priest go would win you cool points with God? Well, it won't! That's not how we win favor with God. God's favor doesn't rest on the slippery slope of how good we have been or in the nobility of our work. By the same token, we don't lose cool points with God for doing the very thing God has called us to do well. While we certainly are afforded a certain amount of discretion and consider situations on a case-by-case basis, why would you write a laborer a ticket for speeding and not write the priest one? God is not a respecter of persons; he doesn't play favorites. There are no big "I's" and little "you's," especially in terms on whom his divine favor rests. God's grace and divine favor rest on those who believe in his son who is Jesus of Nazareth as we shall see below.

With direct reference to our text, (Luke 7:1-10), I want to leave you with two main points for further reflection as it relates to law enforcement officers. The commander in the text models what it means to be a believer in law enforcement. It further illustrates that there is no conflict of interest in embracing our spirituality by humbly and respectfully walking it out for others to see.

Main point #1: We need to know that we can approach God by faith.

Sometimes there are barriers that can deter us from approaching God by faith. As reflected above, because the commander and his one hundred or so officers were not only enforcers of the law but also conquerors of the land, Roman officers were hated by the Jews overall. They didn't hate this particular commander; they hated the perceived system of government and oppression he worked for. However, this commander apparently had an impeccable reputation of strong character among the Jewish elders, as they would later approach the Jewish Jesus on behalf of the commander. The commander was a slave owner and one his servants had become critically ill. I don't know if you have ever watched someone you love dying, but from what I hear, it's agonizing. Sure, there was real tension between Roman soldiers and Jews, but sometimes God will allow our situations to become so dire and hopeless that we have nowhere else to turn *but* to him. Have you ever found yourself in that place? That's certainly the situation this commander found himself in. He was at the miracle-seeking stage and in a life-altering expression of faith, he turned to the Jewish Jesus to seek healing for his servant.

The fact that the commander owned slaves is a nonissue to me. Right or wrong, contextually, people owned slaves during the first century. What seems more important to me, and it seems Jesus felt the same way, is the fact that the text says the servant was "dear" to the commander. Jesus seemed more concerned with the commander's deep love for his servants than him owning slaves. I believe the commander really loved his servant very deeply to approach a Jewish man for help on his behalf, not knowing how he would really be perceived.

Main Point #2: We need to know that we can approach God because of his goodness and Lordship.

God seeks to be good to us because he *is* good. True faith means humbly acknowledging Jesus' Lordship and approaching him on the basis of his goodness and mercy. Somehow, the commander knew that Jesus' willingness and ability to help him and his servant had nothing to do with how good the commander had been or how effective he was at law enforcement. He knew it had everything to do with the fact that Jesus wanted to be good to him and he believed Jesus would. Because of the commander's belief in Jesus' ability to help him, the text says that his servant got healed instantly.

The commander was a man in authority but was willing to humbly submit to the authority and Lordship of Jesus. The commander said something that resonated in my own heart. As Jesus was making his approach to the commander's home, the commander, who showed great humility in his unwillingness to even approach Jesus, sent messengers instead. Just because he believed Jesus would help him doesn't mean he believed he was worthy of the Lord's help. In fact, he had so much faith in Jesus' ability to fix his dire situation that he asserted something that deeply stirred the heart of Jesus. He said that it was unnecessary for Jesus to come to his house, for he believed that Jesus was not bound by time and space in his ability to do the miraculous. That is just what Jesus did in healing the servant, all because of the commander's faith as expressed in his humble submission to the authority and Lordship of Jesus. It moved Jesus deeply, causing him to utter these words: *"I tell you, not even in Israel have I found such faith."* How much more should we follow the commander's example in our willingness to believe we can approach God . . . not because we have been good but because *he* is good?

Afterword
A Prayer of Comfort

God is our refuge and strength, a helper who is always
found in times of trouble
(Psalm 46:1 ESV).

Father God, I greet you in awe of the wonderful works of
your hands in creation. God, I thank you for the gift of life,
liberty, and the ability to pursue happiness. God, I thank you
for being a friend who sticks closer than any brother. Father,
on behalf of the entire law enforcement community, we thank
you for our families and our friends who cry with us, encourage us, love us, and support us. Father, we thank you for your
never-ending forgiveness for our past, present, and future
inequities. Please forgive me and my brothers and sisters in
whatever manner we have fallen short in trying to protect and
serve the community.

Lord, I thank you for the privileged call to law enforcement
for each of us and the honor of serving your people each and
every day. God, I thank you for divine help and strength each
day, especially during the tough times in law enforcement we
must all face. Lord, thank you for using those tough times and
moments to mature and develop us. Father, where would law
enforcement officers be without your steadfast love and cov-
enant care each step of our journey? God, this job is too hard
and too stressful to do without you. I ask that you keep a safe

place for officers in the shadow of your wings that we might run to you for help when we get overwhelmed and bogged down with the cares and worries of life. Lord, thank you for always keeping us safe from hurt, harm, and danger, and from dangers seen and unseen.

God, in a world that is ravaged by evil, we understand that, unfortunately, some of us are called to make the ultimate sacrifice for your greater good and glory. I humbly admit I don't always understand your ways, but, God, I have never doubted the richness and faithfulness of your love for us. God, I pray for strength and comfort for the families of our brothers and sisters who have died in the line of duty so that others in the community may live. Father, please continue to pour out your spirit into the hearts of the law enforcement community. Please send help for the hurting and brokenhearted among us. Father, we trust that you are never blind to our tears, never deaf to our prayers, and never silent to our pain. We are grateful that you are always willing and able to meet our needs by faith if we are willing to humble our hearts enough to ask. Father, may we never lose hope in your ability to sustain us and keep us in the tough days ahead. Please strengthen us all to continue to do your will in our families on the job and in the community. We pray to that end in the name of our Lord . . . Amen!

CPSIA information can be obtained
at www.ICGtesting.com
Printed in the USA
LVHW031742090120
643080LV00005B/758/P